SPORT
IN FOCUS

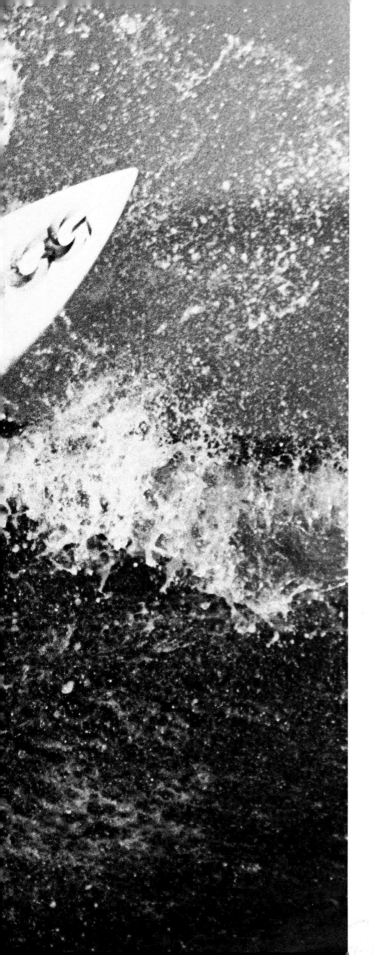

SPORT IN FOCUS

CHRIS SMITH

PARTRIDGE PRESS

Designed by Graeme Murdoch

Text copyright © 1987 by
Sebastian Coe, Dudley Doust,
Brendan Foster, Hugh McIlvanney,
Brough Scott

Photographs copyright © 1987 by Chris Smith
Published in Great Britain by
Partridge Press
Maxwelton House
Boltro Road
Haywards Heath
West Sussex

(Partridge Press is an imprint of
Transworld Publishers Limited
61–63 Uxbridge Road, London W5)

Printed in Great Britain by
BAS Printers Limited
Over Wallop
Hampshire

ISBN 1-85225-001-1

INTRODUCTION
By Sebastian Coe

A WELL-CAPTURED photograph can often tell you more about a sport than a full-length feature film. And even though many of the competitors in this book have been seen a thousand times before, the images provided by such an outstanding photographer as Chris Smith so often have something new to say about them, their achievements and their sport.

I first appreciated the quality of Chris Smith's work in the Sports Council's *Sports Photographer of the Year* competition. Anyone who wins that keenly-contested title no fewer than four times, as Chris has done, is clearly one of the best sports photographers in the business. It takes a great deal more than mere luck to produce the kind of evocative and stimulating pictures which Chris so consistently captures.

All of the photographs in this book were taken in black and white for Sunday newspapers, often in difficult circumstances and frequently against the clock, which on a Saturday afternoon can move so quickly if you are a photographer, yet so slowly if you are an anxious competitor.

There are parallels between the sportsman and the specialist photographer. Both in their own way seek perfection and both are willing to undergo considerable discomfort and inconvenience if it will help to achieve their ultimate target. To be honest, in many ways I would actually rather be

Seb Coe: Olympic Games, Los Angeles 1984

running 10 miles in the wind and rain than standing in it, looking through a viewfinder!

For the athlete standing on the Olympic starting line and the photographer waiting to capture his performance for future generations, there is no second chance. The moment is now, and in both cases the adrenaline flows. And while the competitor cannot be aware of the photographer at that precise second, he is surely grateful for the care and determination which shows so clearly in the subsequent results of the photographer's art. It is always a pleasure to be able to admire the work of a man like Chris who is able to reflect so distinctively, through his camera, the triumphs and the disappointments.

Blessed with a remarkable eye for striking images and interesting relationships, and armed with technical brilliance, Chris gives in this book a unique account of sport in the modern era. Seen singly over breakfast on a Sunday morning, these photographs were striking. Seen together, they form a celebration of everything for which sport exists. Newspapers are alarmingly ephemeral, yet these photographs deserved a more permanent home. Fortunately this book is able to provide that home, and with it a lasting record of 20 oustanding years in sports photo-journalism. Chris Smith is not just a man who loves his work, he also loves sport.

Sebastian Coe

Graeme Souness and Mick Robinson:
Rome 1984

Right, Roma Fans: European Cup Final,
Rome 1984

Biathlon: Olympic Games, Lake Placid 1980

Paul Mariner: Highbury 1984

George Best and Mike England: White Hart
Lane 1973

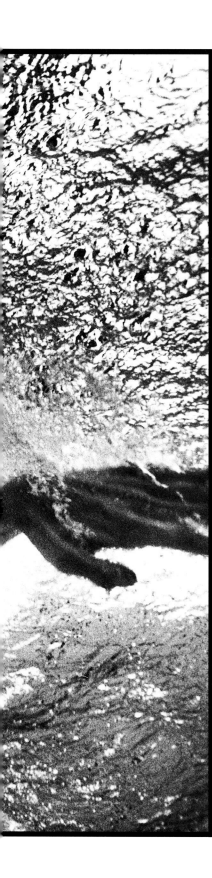

Steve Grossman: Crystal Palace 1971

Top, Peter Winterbottom: Twickenham 1982

Jean Pierre Rives: Parc des Princes 1981

Top, Bill Beaumont: Twickenham 1979

David Duckham and Gerald Davies:
Twickenham 1974

Steve Smith and Terry Holmes: Cardiff 1983

HUGH McILVANNEY

DISPATCHES FROM THE RING

THE TRUISM that professional boxing is like no other sport is reinforced by just about every photograph ever taken of a fighter at work. Desperate moments in other games can, when frozen by the camera, translate into beautiful abstractions. Even the most violent collision of American football players, the kind of battering impact that sends an 18-stone athlete cartwheeling several feet above the turf, can look innocently balletic when the masked and padded figures are suspended in tableau within a 10 inches by 5 inches rectangle on a sports page. But there is seldom the remotest illusion of anything ethereal in pictures of fighters. The business of the ring is so relentlessly concerned with the direct assault of one man upon another's body and spirit (without any diluting distractions like a ball or a stopwatch or a measuring tape) that no glimpse of it can ever be totally devoid of a sense of hazard and apprehension./*continued*

Muhammad Ali: Las Vegas 1980

Clearly, nothing in the assertions just made challenges the obvious fact that many of the very best boxing photographs are entirely free of violence. They may sometimes have an almost eerie quality of repose. But they are always dispatches from the front, always narratives of some sort. The story they suggest may be simply one of pride or hope but more often the human sagas hinted at in these outstanding pictures from the fight game deal with pain or vulnerability, with spirits under bombardment or dreams already broken.

Whether you are drawn to it or repelled by it, there is no denying that boxing is in the end the most dramatic of all the activities that are classed as sport. More than that, it is the hardest – physically and pyschologically. So it is natural, indeed inevitable, that the most compelling of its images should be poignant and frequently bleak. For proof, look no further than the photographs of Howard Winstone and Barry McGuigan, of Johnny Owen and, yes, of Muhammad Ali that appear on the pages of this book.

Nobody ever looked through a lens and saw fighters and their trade more honestly or more movingly than Chris Smith does. He sees them first, last and always as people. Sometimes they are people doing well, having a good time, as Ali certainly is in the fish-eye shot of him addressing an enthralled throng in a hall behind Caesars Palace Hotel in Las Vegas. But more often they are people under stress, in crisis, as Barry McGuigan so blatantly is in the picture which shows those wide, attractive eyes pitifully drained of all that bubbling, mischievous energy that is the everyday currency of his nature.

Now and then the message is less direct but tightens the throat just the same. That is surely the case with the smiling study of Johnny Owen. It would be both false and insulting to claim that the sight of that elongated, alarmingly thin torso, of the spindly arms and the child-like face perched on the long neck, gave warning of the horrors that awaited this tragic boy in a grubby, tumultuous arena in downtown Los Angeles. Equally, however, it is impossible to look on Johnny Owen as rendered by Chris Smith without feeling that this 24-year-old, who was still a virgin (and not merely in the sexual sense) when he went into the ring to challenge a fierce Mexican called Lupe Pintor for the world bantamweight championship in September of 1980, never belonged in such hostile company.

The fight ended dreadfully in the 12th round, with the young Welshman plunged into a coma that led inexorably to death in the first week of November. A piece I filed to *The Observer* a few hours after the knockout has a sentence that reads: 'There is something about his pale face, with its large nose, jutting ears and uneven teeth, all set above that long, skeletal frame, that takes hold of the heart and makes unbearable the thought of him being badly hurt.' I cannot glance at Chris's picture without finding all the anxiety I carried into the Olympic Auditorium on that Friday night welling up anew. Yet the smile, with its strange mixture of shyness and comfortable acceptance of his revealing pose, reminds me that Johnny Owen was immeasurably more at ease in the milieu of boxing than in any other area of his short life. The final few words of that sad report from Los Angeles said: 'Outside the ring he was an inaudible and almost invisible personality. Inside, he became astonishingly positive and self-assured. He seemed to be more at home there than anywhere else. It is his tragedy that he found himself articulate in such a dangerous language.'

It is natural that several of the boxing pictures in this book should cause uneasy stirrings in someone like myself who finds the game nearly irresistible but remains incurably ambivalent about its ultimate validity in a civilised society. Asking just how civilised modern society (with its soaring crime rates, corruption at all levels and perennial threat of nuclear annihilation) is supposed to be may emphasise that the legitimacy of public fisticuffs is a long way from being the most pressing issue of the day. But it doesn't neutralise the disturbing effect of an unflinching though unmistakably sympathetic record of the ordeals of fighting men.

Some of these photographs are so inspired, so striking that they almost demand to be hung on a gallery wall but there was nothing arty about Chris Smith's approach to shooting them. On the contrary, their power might be traced, in part at least, to habits and perceptions he developed as the distinguished, prize-winning news photographer he was before he began piling up awards for the coverage of sport. He is a master of composition but the flow of feeling through his pictures is almost invariably more important than the deployment of shapes, human or inanimate. For him, timing is seldom merely a matter of capturing a climax of movement. Frequently, and particularly when fighters are his subject, it is the moment of maximum intensity, or maximum significance, he is seeking to imprison.

The stunning series encompassing a decade of Muhammad Ali's incomparable career – from the preparation for his first historic and heroic collision with Joe Frazier in 1971 to the miserable occasion in 1980 when a compassionate Larry Holmes toyed with the leftovers of Ali's greatness – stresses that criterion. So does the shot of Colin Jones slumping open-mouthed against a ring post after being lacerated by the devastatingly sharp punching of Donald Curry and, less dramatically but no less tellingly, so does the beautiful study of Curry at work on the speed ball. Sheffield's Herol Graham posing against the background of a steelworks in his home town is a classy example of what Chris would call a bit of fun. But the pictures of Howard Winstone (like that heartbreaking moment from the fight that cost Barry McGuigan his world featherweight title in Las Vegas and destroyed his relationship with his manager, Barney Eastwood) are all seriousness.

In the action shot, Winstone tries with one good eye to keep track of the harmful intentions of Jose Legra, who is about to relieve Howard of a version of the world championship that magnificent Welsh boxer held for six months in 1968. The other shows Winstone, bulging slightly in his waistcoat and with the dregs of a half-pint of Guinness at his elbow, in a pub reverie about the might-have-beens of a career in which all the wonders of his technique and the beauty of his spirit in the ring were thwarted by the superior physical strength of the remarkable Mexican who was the supreme featherweight of the mid-Sixties – Vicente Saldivar.

It is an irony not untypical of boxing that, after fighting forty-odd rounds against Saldivar and being unlucky to be denied the verdict in one of their three matches, Winstone should have been battered into retirement by Legra, who wasn't in the Mexican's league. Of course, Howard brought only the worn remnants of his gifts to that sad occasion at a Porthcawl fairground in the summer of 1968. My friendship with Winstone and his manager Eddie Thomas (two Merthyr Tydfil men I like and admire as much as anyone I have ever met in connection with boxing) enabled me to engineer for Chris Smith the privilege of shooting pictures of Howard before he went into the ring against Legra. Chris appreciated that edge, since the opportunity to photograph fighters in the hour or so before a contest is infinitely rarer than the chance to train the camera on them after they have won or lost. He wanted to make the most of his opening and in my anxiety to help him I suggested that perhaps he would like me to persuade Winstone to stay near the one naked light bulb that illuminated the champion's squalidly inadequate 'dressing room.'

Chris is a polite, even a gentle man but as a working-class lad from Hartlepool he can bring strong hints of iron to the surface now and again and this was one time when I, having made the crass error of interrupting his work, was given a glimpse of his harder side. 'Hugh, I'm very grateful to you for getting me in here,' he said, 'but now would you piss off and let me get on with this.'

Let me stress that I am not usually so rash about poking my nose into the business of other professionals, least of all that of photographers. The cameramen I have worked with on a regular basis during my years in Fleet Street have been of a calibre to discourage such folly. In the early days with *The Observer* there were Stuart Heydinger and Gerry Cranham, two utterly different men linked by exceptional talent. And over the last 20 years or so I have been permitted to go about my job in the company of first Chris Smith and then Eamonn McCabe and if that isn't privileged treatment I'd like to know what is. In addition to turning out pictures of often breathtaking brilliance (the kind which, as I have acknowledged in the past, can make a sportswriter feel that his function is to produce 1500-word captions), Eamonn and Chris are stalwart companions to have on the road and more than bright enough to enlarge or correct the perceptions of any writer they are operating with.

It is Eamonn who is my *Observer* ally these days, of course, while Chris is in the opposition camp of *The Sunday Times* but anyone who thinks that must make a difference to how Smith and I get along with each other doesn't know much about us. It's not crazy to suggest that Chris Smith can be used as a sort of litmus test when assessing other people in our trade. If somebody doesn't like Chris, or Chris doesn't like him or her (and that's a rarity), then I for one wouldn't be in any rush to head for the bar with the individual in question.

When Chris Smith and I get together – and since both of us have pitched up in Richmond in southwest London that's not a desperately unusual occurrence – the reminiscences of strange working days shared are likely to come in a flood capable of numbing the minds of family or friends foolish enough to remain within earshot. The events surrounding my 40th birthday on Haiti (which fell during a visit to the training camp of the island's World Cup footballers) can keep us going for a while. Then there is the tale of an expedition to the small racetrack at Bowie in Maryland to see Chris McCarron, who was then in the process of making himself the most successful apprentice in the history of horse racing and has since become one of the outstanding riders in the game, with dramatic achievements in the American Triple Crown races of 1987 to emphasise that status. Young McCarron was in splendid form when we met up with him but the same could hardly be said of Smith or myself. We had flown down from New

York after an excessively congenial evening among old acquaintances in Manhattan and neither the photographer nor the scribbler found it too easy to make one brain cell connect with another around breakfast time. However, as the day progressed a semblance of mental vigour was restored and our duties were fairly competently discharged.

But the experience was a stiff reminder to both of us that, quite apart from avoiding the sauce at all costs while on the job, those in our business are well advised to keep away from it on the night before anything other than the most trivial assignment. Mind you, it is a relevant fact that in Manhattan bars the night before can last until 4am.

Some of the most pleasant and amusing memories Chris and I share are drawn from several days we spent around Muhammad Ali in Miami early in 1971. Ali, recently returned to boxing at the end of the three-and-a-half year exile imposed on him because of his refusal to be drafted, was preparing for his first fight with Joe Frazier. He was soon to move to New York to be exposed to the traditional media mob scene but American reporters and broadcasters, who are even more powerfully influenced by herd instincts than are their counterparts on this side of the Atlantic, were disinclined to pay any attention to the final phase of his Miami training. So Chris and I had the genius almost to ourselves for nearly a week.

Often the only other presence was Reggie Thomas, a Black Muslim agent from Chicago who was acting as chauffeur and bodyguard to Ali at the time. Reggie was quite a presence. Small and light-skinned, with the deliberately composed features and mobile eyes of the professional bodyguard, he favoured single-colour ensembles (usually white or blue) from his flat cap to this pull-on boots. It was always safe to assume that he was also wearing something metal and highly functional.

In the still hour between five and six o'clock on those Miami mornings, Reggie was to be found easing a black Cadillac around the three-mile perimeter of Bayshore golf course behind the loping figure of his employer. Once while we were in the car a small dog of vaguely terrier origin suddenly scurried towards Ali with a yelping show of aggression and the man from Chicago, responding to the imperatives of his trade and his nature, put his foot on the accelerator with every intention of obliterating the threat. 'Hey, Reggie, leave him alone,' shouted Muhammad. 'He don't mean nothin'. He just a bluff dog.'

Soon Muhummad had tired of running, which he invariably did earlier than he should, and began to scan the pre-dawn sky for signs of the fleet of spacecraft whose unique propensities were at that time providing one of the more arresting themes of his monologues. These craft were apparently patrolling the heavens on behalf of the wronged black peoples of the earth, ready to visit a terrible retribution on the whites if they failed to abandon their persecuting ways. The smaller machines were, Ali told us, equipped with three-pound jack-hammer bombs that could, if required, burrow underground and set off subterranean explosions that would topple cities. The mother ship of the fleet could 'travel at 18,000 miles an hour and turn on a pinhead.' Even Ali's imagination checked its stride momentarily when confronted with that capability.

'I don't know what turning like that does to the people inside the mother ship but I suppose the wise men in the east have figured that out.' A little later he left me just a shade disconcerted by asking: 'How much does the world weigh?' But he immediately let me off the hook: 'You won't know – you white guys weren't around when they gave out that information.'

In addition to the simple pleasure of those episodes (the joyful sense of fun with which all of them were imbued), they were touched with a hint of wonder and mystery – filled as they were with the magical ambiguity of the young Ali's spirit, in which conscious mischief and a genuine surrealist extravagance so compellingly mingled. Experiencing at first-hand the glorious originality of Muhammad Ali has been one of the enduring delights and satisfactions of my professional life. And, like much of the best that has happened to me as a journalist, it has been further enriched by being shared with Chris Smith. □

Right, Johnny Owen: Tredegar 1980

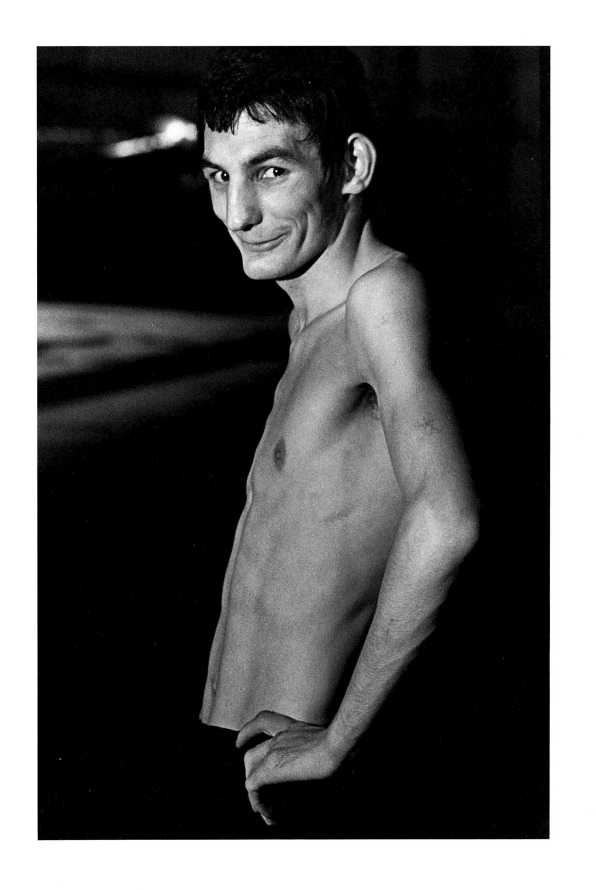

Barry McGuigan: Commonwealth Games,
Edmonton 1978

Right, Barry McGuigan: Las Vegas 1986

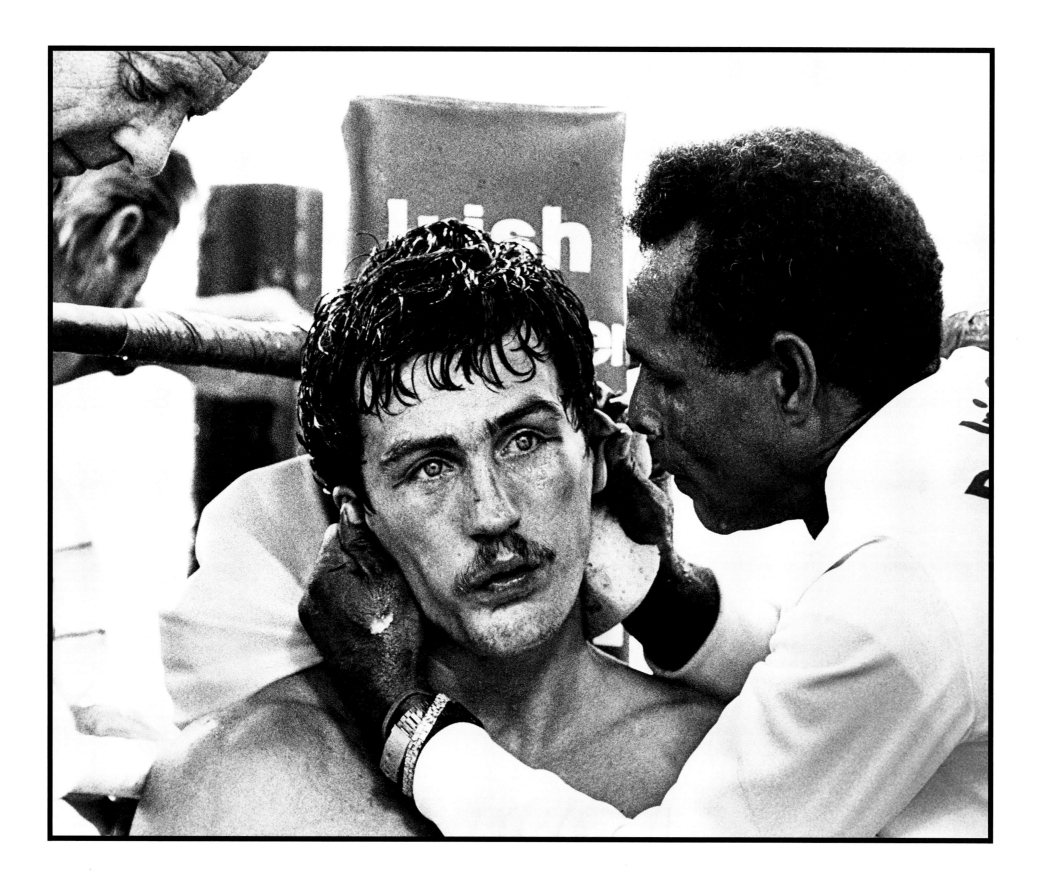

Howard Winstone: Robertstown 1978

Left, Howard Winstone v Jose Legra:
Porthcawl 1968

Above, Don Curry: Miami 1985

Right, Colin Jones v Don Curry: Birmingham
1986

Herol Graham: Sheffield 1985

Left, Marvin Hagler: Las Vegas 1987

Muhammad Ali v Joe Frazier : Madison
Square Garden 1971

Right, Muhammad Ali : 5th Street Gym,
Miami 1971

Muhammad Ali v Larry Holmes: Las Vegas
1980

Frank Bruno v Tim Witherspoon: Wembley
1986

Left, Frank Bruno: Canning Town 1986

Above and right, Mike Tyson: Las Vegas
1987

Round the Island Race: Cowes 1981

Jimmy Rimmer: Highbury 1984

David Duckham : Twickenham 1973

Tour de France : Bordeaux 1977

Coxed Fours:
Henley Regatta 1985

Left, Long Jump:
Commonwealth Games,
Brisbane 1982

Vassily Alexeyev: Olympic
Games, Moscow 1980

Skiing: Val d' Isere 1986

Right, Wild Water Championships:
Llangollen 1982

Admiral's Cup : Cowes 1986

DUDLEY DOUST

Off-The-Ball Art

Jack Nicklaus:
Open Championship, Sandwich 1981

THE WONDERFUL thing about Chris Smith's pictures of golfers is that they aren't about golf. That is to say they aren't – or at least most of them aren't – about the moment a shot has been struck. Seldom in one of his golf photographs will you see the splash of sand, a divot floating up from a fairway or the twisted look on a player's face as he pounds a ball from a tee.

Why is this so wonderful? Because, at least to my way of thinking, the bigger and more revealing truths surrounding this strange and ancient game, the *pangs*, have little to do with the act of hitting a ball. Or, for that matter, with returning a fine or an ugly score. Rather, to borrow a term used in soccer, the game's truths are disclosed 'off the ball.' They come during the gaps between shots, the 95-odd per cent of the stressful-contemplative time spent on the course while in pursuit of what the great Bobby Jones once called 'a game of consider-

able passion, either of the explosive type, or that which burns inwardly and sears the soul.'

A soul-searing sport. Jones, for a lawyer, had a nice poetic ear for a pastime that is fundamentally simple. To enjoy it a player needs neither partner nor opponent although, even in adulthood, one and the same seem to clank alongside the player on your appointed rounds. Furthermore, the object of the game is daft, and one I feel must be antipathic to the stingy Scots, those probable perpetrators of the game. It goes: the less you play – that is the fewer times you hit the ball – the better your results.

Golf was the first game to grip me and I wish Chris had travelled with me years ago at the Tecumseh golf course, now sadly disappearing into the bulldozer's maw, near my native American city of Syracuse, New York. It would have been a tough photographic challenge to capture my passions and fantasies as I trudged down those fairways which during the war were often thick with unmown neglect. Could he have caught my dreams of driving past the spreading oak tree on the second hole, or my nightmare terror of hitting into the ball-swallowing rough only one hole from the end? Somehow, I suspect he probably could.

I can claim to know something about golf, having covered the game with intermittent regularity – if you will allow such a term – since Arnold Palmer won the Masters tournament in Georgia in 1960. I know, for example, that you should never pluck your club from your bag until you are ready to play; the freshness of anticipation drains dead in your hands. I know that when playing your drive off the 14th hole at St. Andrews you should sight off the church steeple in town; otherwise your ball may end up in one of the four invisible Beardies bunkers. I know, too, that the former dictator of the Phillipines, Ferdinand Marcos, cheats at golf. I once saw him fiddle-up a fairway lie at the Wack Wack club outside Manila.

For himself, Chris Smith will admit to knowing less about golf than he does other sports. However, he certainly understands the loneliness and lucid *longueurs* that light up the game. Who else, for example, has so dramatically captured the sense of disgust and frustration over a poor performance, one hacked out of a nagging rain, than Chris did when he photographed the scowling Severiano Ballesteros during the 1985 Open championship at Sandwich. The picture, felicitously called the Golfing Matador, indeed illustrates Jones's passion 'which burns inwardly and sears the soul.'

The story behind the picture, to digress briefly, demonstrates how professionally Chris meets the demands of photo-journalism. It was taken during the second round of the championship – on a Friday, if you please, for a Sunday newspaper. It was made as a 'holding' picture meant to be replaced the following afternoon by a more newsy shot of the tournament leader. On that Friday Chris had chosen to follow Seve, the defending champion, not only because Ballesteros is dependably photogenic but because the following morning I was to write a feature-report on the Spaniard who was hopelessly trailing the leaders. The package, picture and story, could be wrapped up tidily by first edition time. Smith dogged Seve all that second day and, during a sudden downpour of rain he got his picture.

It was a stunner. To the unknowing observer, such as myself, it appears that Seve is wearing his waterproof as a bullfighter's cape. He isn't. He actually is pulling it across his chest. His motion is so swift that in only one frame of Smith's 'take' does the waterproof look like a cape. Chris knew this. He knew he had the shot – he always seems to know what he's got, even before he processes his film – and needless to say the photograph was safely in London by Saturday morning and ran through all editions of the paper. It was to win a prize as the best black-and-white golf picture of the year and earned Seve's acclaim. 'Good photograph,' the Spaniard said later, smiling grimly at it. 'It says how I felt. It makes me remember.'

Smith's pictures indeed coax out memories and by absorbing yourself in the rich reproductions over the following pages you get an inkling of what painterly mastery he has brought to the art of sports photography. They are all black-and-white. Chris works almost exclusively in black-and-white, not only because that is the imposed language of newspaper photo-journalism, but because it brings a feeling of urgency to even the most tranquil of his still-lifes.

*   *   *   *   *

Chris Smith's first picture for *The Sunday Times* appeared on January 9, 1977. I know because I was with him on the story. We travelled to Pedreña in northern Spain where he made his memorable – and later to be much-copied – photograph of the emerging superstar of golf, Seve Ballesteros, then only 19 years old. This picture, taken against the distant background of the Royal Golf Club of Pedreña, shows the young Spaniard playing a practice shot off the beach of the Bay of Santander. It tells an interesting and unlaboured story. Seve, you see, grew up less than privileged in a farmhouse on the edge of the course and as caddy was banned from practicing on the club's exclusive grounds. Consequently, fired by resentment and desire, he went with his friends to the beach where he honed the gifts he later would wreak upon the world.

As a vehicle for this rags-to-riches tale, the picture was spot on. It certainly helped my story, but then Chris's pictures *always* help a writer; that's one reason why we seek his company on the newspaper. Yet to admire the picture for this reason alone is selfish, patronising and journalistically one-eyed, rather like introducing Chris to a subject as 'my photographer' or 'our photographer.' Seve on the Beach has multiple merits of its own.

Firstly and simply, the picture is technically satisfying. Notice the fine detail of the footprints in the foreground. They are messy perhaps and some photographers would have raked them out. Smith left them there to soften the sense of portraiture and give a casual, man-at-work air to the picture. What's more, by accident or design, the scruffy sand adds another layer of visual depth to the composition. Notice, too, the dimples on the golf balls in the sand and the texture of yonder clouds. Chris, as other photographers are quick to point out, 'knows how to use light.' This is a *good* picture. Beyond this, Seve on the Beach is just about a perfect expression of what has become a trademark of a Smith photograph: the Figure in a Landscape.

Figures in Landscapes. In sports photography they probably lend themselves to golf more intrinsically than to any other sport except perhaps mountain-climbing. The reason is obvious. Golf is played across landscape (and over seascape) which usually is beautiful, and is it not difficult to take a passable shot of the rocky, sea-torn 16th at Cypress Point? Or Turnberry with the lighthouse in the distance? Chris's figures and landscapes go

much deeper than this. Two other pictures spring to mind.

One is of Neil Coles. That marvellous British figure of the sixties and seventies, probably the most under-rated golfer of his day because he was loath to travel to and test himself in America, is seen strolling across two bald, interlocking hillocks. He wears a preoccupied look on his face. In his hand a club swings idly but with the pure beat of a metronome. This *is* Neil Coles. Anyone who knows him, or whoever watched him, will sense this with a feeling of truth and warmth. Neil Coles was a loner and possessed of the most rhythmic swing in golf. Smith has laid these singular traits against the most lovely and unobtrusive of landscapes. I wonder if Chris knows how good this picture is.

The third of these Figures in a Landscape is the backshot of Jack Nicklaus toiling up a sandhill. It appears to have been taken from far away but to accentuate the figure, puts him on a dome of his own so to speak, Chris used a 'fish-eye' lens and was only a few feet behind Nicklaus when he made the shot. In my view it is one of the finest candid sports photographs ever taken. If art is controlled accident, this picture is it. Everything in it, either sought by Smith or happily haphazard, comes together at once simply and complex. Firstly, the setting is unmistakable but lies just at the edge of your memory: it is a visually special Open links, St. George's at Sandwich, where the lack of feature is a unique feature of its own. Under those clouds piled up over the English Channel you can all but hear the 'larks singing as they seem to sing nowhere else,' as Bernard Darwin, the greatest of golf writers, observed as long ago as 1910.

Nearer to hand, the figure is unmistakably

Nicklaus, alone and resolute, tired and somehow a little down in the shoulders. Aged 41, he appears to be climbing some Final Hill towards some terminal, allegorical Flag. See the tiny figures on the horizon: the Golden Bear indeed was a giant among pigmies. In context the photograph was particularly poignant. Nicklaus had scored an 83 in his first round, the worst in his Open career, a performance which unknown to us at the time had without doubt been affected by the news from home that one of his sons had been involved in a serious road accident. The Golden Bear had persevered through the championship, however, and his domestic news had just broken to the public when Smith's photograph appeared on Sunday morning. It was a deeply powerful picture.

In the following folio there are other photographs that stir a range of emotions – Tony Jacklin, eyes closed and cheeks puffed in fatigue on the winning green at the 1969 Open at Royal Lytham and St. Annes is one – and which looked so journalistically timely when they first appeared. Days later they still looked fresh as they peered up crookedly out of dustbins and now, at last, they are held safe between hard covers. I could talk about all of them. Have a good look; they represent subtle golf photography, off-the-ball and at its best. □

Seve Ballesteros: Pedreña 1977

Right, Seve Ballesteros: Open Championship,
Sandwich 1985

Tony Jacklin: Open Championships,
Royal Lytham St Annes 1979

Tony Jacklin: Ryder Cup, The Belfry 1986

Clive Clark and Fans: Stoke Poges 1968

Neil Coles: Moor Allerton 1982

Lee Trevino: Wentworth 1972

Arnold Palmer: Augusta 1987

Greg Norman: Wentworth 1985

Right, Ryder Cup: The Belfry 1986

Skiing : Crans Montana 1987

Left, Luge : Olympic Games, Sarajevo 1984

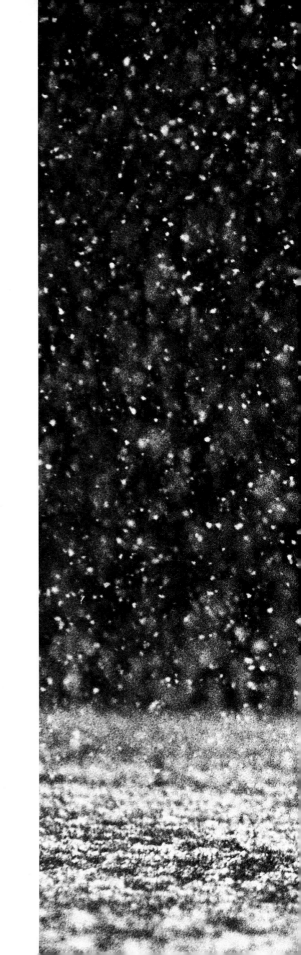

World Cup: Spain 1982

Football: Highbury 1979

Greyhound Racing: Hackney 1986

Biathlon: Olympic Games, Sarajevo 1984

Widnes v Wigan: Wembley 1984

Featherstone Rovers v Warrington : Wembley
1974

Muhammad Ali: Miami 1971

Devizes to Westminster Race: 1980

Alan Wells:
Olympic Games, Moscow 1980

BRENDAN FOSTER

ONLY THE BEST

Dave Moorcroft:
Olympic Games, Los Angeles 1984

ATHLETICS, I keep hearing, has changed. Even during the span captured so graphically in this book, many people have become convinced that the influx of money to the participants is some-how altering the very nature of track and field. Of course, it wasn't like that in your day, they hint with knowing looks. But they are wrong. And they would still be wrong if they were talking to Harold Abrahams, Dorando Pietri or the participants in the ancient Olympic Games.

The sideshows may alter. But through its extreme simplicity, the sport and its competitors have not changed one scrap. Look at the bottled-up determination on the faces of Alan Wells and his opponents at the start of their 100 metres heat at the 1980 Moscow Olympics. What you see are not the expressions of athletes pre-occupied with money, sponsorship, or anything other than the basic animal instinct of wanting to get to the finish before anyone else. That instinct has been ascribed in the past as being the need of Man the Hunter to find food for his family. If that need no longer remains, the instinct does, and is given vent in competition. An athlete whose prime motivation is anything other than the competitive urge is likely to have been eliminated from the reckoning long before he reaches the Olympic arena.

At the Seoul Olympics in 1988, the basic nature of what Chris Smith sees through his viewfinder will be little different from what he would have seen had he been covering the first modern Olympics in Athens in 1896. The surroundings, the clothing, the rules, might have been different. The competitive fire would not.

The pursuit, the anticipation and the celebration of victory are so often the making of a good athletics photograph. But often defeat and disappointment can tell an equally vivid story when you know how much someone wanted to win. For me, one of the most graphic moments on these pages is that of Dave Moorcroft in the 1984 Los Angeles Olympic 5,000 metres final. As world record holder for the event, he had overcome persistent injury and illness to reach the Games, apparently in excellent form. But a groin injury affected him before the final. He refused a pain-killing injection, choosing to run the race anyway. At first sight in the picture, he seems to be leading into the home straight, well clear. But on closer examination you can see the eventual winner, Said Aouita of Morocco, behind Dave, already acknowledging victory. Dave is almost a lap in arrears and in great pain, yet refusing to drop out, as he so easily could have done. Sometimes the man is almost too brave for his own good. Yet his attitude was that he would try to do the best he could on the day which mattered, instead of just abandoning the task.

Seeing a photograph of myself in the Olympic arena – leading a 5,000 metres heat in the controversially-designed Montreal Stadium in 1976 – evokes a curious sensation. My own competitive career is now a closed chapter, so to see myself in action, whether in a photograph or on video, is almost like looking at a different person, But I can remember the occasion clearly, because the competitive peak to which an athlete aimed always remained a vivid recollection. Whether it ended in success or failure, you can always recall how you felt as you walked slowly out of the stadium, numb with disappointment, or ran a victory lap on air almost as fast as the race itself.

Sometimes an unexpected loss is attributed to overmuch pressure on the athlete, and it is suggested by some that this pressure may be greater than ever now. But the truly competitive athlete feels pressure only from himself – and that is no greater or no less than it always was. If an athlete reacts to what is said about him in the newspapers or on television, or is overly concerned about what *might* be said about him, then he is not in complete control of his own destiny. Regardless of what may be hinted to the contrary, a losing athlete has not let down his public, his country or anything else. He may even be rightly proud of his own losing performance if he feels he has given everything he could.

The very nature of an individual pursuit like athletics can make it a very lonely sport at times. Preparing for a single top-level peak in distance running, for example, involves many hundreds of training runs in all weathers, often twice a day, and frequently alone. The picture of Steve Cram training along Hadrian's Wall, far from the screaming crowds, reflects the isolation very well and is far more a part of the real life of Steve Cram than breaking world records in foreign stadiums. For the public and the media are not with you on those long, fatiguing, uncomfortable runs, when you would much rather be sitting in front of a warm fire watching television.

So while the athlete very much appreciates the support and interest at the big occasions, the real pressure he feels comes from within. I used to have a particularly nervous stomach before major races, but although it was a confounded nuisance on occasions (and I almost missed the start of the 1976 Olympic 10,000 metres because I was in the toilets!), I am satisfied that it was caused by my anxiety about my own performance and not by any anxiety about what anyone else would *think* of my performance.

I do not miss the competition now, perhaps because I am finding business life caters for my inner drive. Looking back, I sometimes wonder exactly what it was that kept me going for so long. I know I was naturally competitive, and that each year from 1970 to 1980 I was ranked No 1 in Britain at whichever event I specialised that season. But why did I continue at such a level for so long, week after week, year after year, with no real break? Why, for instance, weren't five seasons enough?

At the time, not winning an Olympic gold medal and having to settle for a bronze in 1976 was a frustration because it remained the one achievement which eluded me. But in retrospect it perhaps also left me with the will to strive for something else after the end of my running career, and it probably helped me to take some of my hunger pangs into business life afterwards.

I am still able to enjoy some close links with

international athletics through my friendship with Steve Cram. But I remind him constantly that nothing he will ever do in his life afterwards will have quite the same emotional excitement as being in that arena, racing for Olympic gold, and that he should make the most of it while he can: life inevitably moves on for all of us.

They say that if you cannot do the racing yourself, then coaching is second best and commentating on the race is the third. Through my BBC TV commentaries I am at least enjoying the second and third best activities. But after commentating on races, I find myself asking Steve to confirm whether in the Eighties, runners still feel as I did in the Seventies. In a 1,500 metres race, for example, if the first lap was run in a slow 67 seconds I recall how such a pace used to make me nervous and uncomfortable, whereas a time of around 57 seconds felt much more suitable. For while the essence of the sport remains constant, attitudes change. And so does apparent domination.

The picture of Steve Ovett at his unhappiest, during the Los Angeles Olympics, reminds me that he once seemed truly invincible. At the 1977 World Cup final in Düsseldorf and at the 1978 European Championships in Prague, he won the 1,500 metres titles with such unpressed ease against some of the world's greatest runners, that I wondered how anyone could ever beat him. Athletes do go through spells when they are literally unbeatable. Cram has, Ovett has, Sebastian Coe has. And the way that the little Ethiopian of indeterminate age, Miruts Yifter, sprinted away from the 5,000 and 10,000 metres fields at the 1980 Olympic Games made you doubt whether anyone could beat that type of finish. There were even times during my own career when I felt I was ready for anyone in the world. But we all lost races afterwards.

Until the 1987 World Championships in Rome, the athlete who best bore the air of invincibility must have been Daley Thompson. Until then he had been unbeaten in nine years at the decathlon, where there are so many more possibilities for error and defeat than in the average athletic event. He was really the master of producing the goods on the big day. Athletics is full of people who were fit at the wrong time or who earned a single gold medal through being fit at the right time once. But Daley, until Rome, had time and again proved himself, none more so that at the 1986 European Championships in Stuttgart against his two biggest rivals, Jurgen Hingsen and Siggi Wentz. If ever they had a chance to beat him at his best, it was there then, in front of their home crowd. Yet they could not overcome the intense competitiveness of a man who at Seoul in 1988 will surely, until Rome, again prove himself to be the best all-round athlete of all time. Eventually, though, someone will come along who, will make his record performances appear rather tame in comparison. But that is not to say that the athlete will be greater, any more than you can say that Lasse Viren was a greater athlete than Paavo Nurmi, although he ran faster. Both men were prodigious Olympic title winners.

For many people athletics really comes alive when two truly great performers in the same event are competing in the same era, swapping records and titles, and both intent on the No. 1 spot. Often, one athlete may dominate his or her event on a global scale, but a situation like the rivalry between Sebastian Coe and Steve Ovett a few years ago, later joined as third partner by Steve Cram, has done a great deal towards helping to promote the public interest in the sport, both in the UK and elsewhere.

I must admit that I never expected the women's javelin to have a gripping effect, but the similarly intense rivalry between Tessa Sanderson and Fatima Whitbread has forced the event into the spotlight. The picture on the rostrum at the Los Angeles Olympics, shows them in a friendly mood after Tessa took the gold and Fatima the bronze (or is Fatima actually punching Tessa on the jaw?), but they have had their ups and downs since then. In July 1986 it was Tessa, by then the underdog, who unexpectedly took the Commonwealth Games title from Fatima. A month later, with Tessa injured, it was Fatima who not only won the European Championships gold medal in Stuttgart, but also broke the world record into the bargain. What is more, she retained her supremacy into 1987 when at Rome she took the world gold.

These were not just two girls trying to be the best in Britain; they were also trying to be the best in the world: the Olympic champion versus the world record holder. No amount of money could make them more intensely competitive than they already are. Which brings me back to my opening point. Athletes like Tessa and Fatima, or Steve and Seb, may be extremely well known to the public through television and they may be highly paid for endorsements and appearances. But neither of these considerations can help them one iota when they are in the competitive arena. For if you take away the trimmings, it is still simply athlete versus athlete. It always was. And it always will be.   □

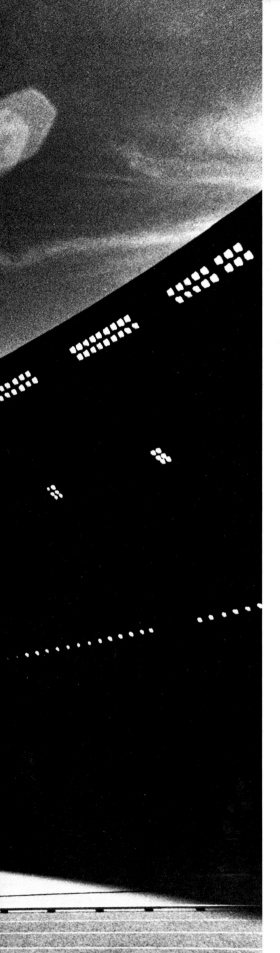

5000 Metres: Olympic Games, Montreal 1976

High Jump: Commonwealth Games,
Brisbane 1982

Left, Miruts Yifter: Olympic Games,
Moscow 1980

Steve Ovett: Olympic Games, Moscow 1980

Steve Cram: Hadrian's Wall 1981

Daley Thompson: Olympic Games, Los Angeles 1984

Tessa Sanderson and Fatima Whitbread:
Olympic Games, Los Angeles 1984

Steeplechase: Olympic Games, Moscow 1980

Linford Christie: Crystal Palace 1987

Carl Lewis and Fans : Olympic Games, Los
Angeles 1984

Four-Man Bob: Olympic Games, Sarajevo
1984

Left, Cyclo-cross: World Championship,
Crystal Palace 1973

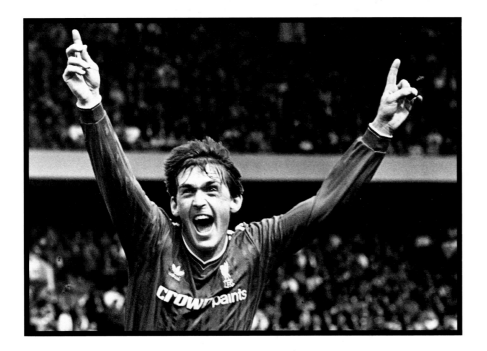

Kenny Dalglish: Stamford Bridge 1986

Joe Jordan: Spain 1982

Paolo Rossi: Spain 1982

Brian Talbot and Frank Stapleton: Wembley
1979

Right, Manchester United Fans: Wembley
1978

Muhammad Ali: Miami 1971

Sugar Ray Leonard: Hilton Head Island 1987

Racing: Newmarket 1972

Adrian Moorhouse: Leeds 1984

Right, Sand Yachting: Pembroke 1982

Phil Mahre: World Championships,
Schladming 1983

Left, Fidelis Obikwu: Commonwealth
Games, Brisbane 1982

BROUGH SCOTT

WINNERS' EXPOSURE

T HE GIFT is of sight. And it's not always easy. Like when we went to the racetrack in Ireland and found it under the sea. Sure, we had been warned about Laytown, 40 miles down the coast from Dublin, the last of the once-frequent beach meetings retain official status. But it was still quite a shaker to reach the appointed 'strand' some four hours before the first race to find boats bobbing in the ocean where the course was supposed to be. 'Don't worry,' said a massive local who was hammering what turned out to be the winning post into sand above the tide, 'she'll be going out fast in a minute.'

The next few hours blurred into some wonderful Celtic celebration of King Canute in reverse. As the sea rolled back, the marker posts went in, the crowds came out, the horses began to arrive and the racegoers included at least one white-ankled holy sister paddling alongside two gentle inmates

Racing on the Strand:
Leytown, Ireland 1977

from the shore side asylum rather charmingly referred to as 'the giggle factory.' The images flocked in thick and fast enough to fill a couple of books for starters. For Chris Smith it had to be just one picture. Faced with this dilemma there are two normal reactions. To lens away at everything and hope a good picture comes along, or to decide firmly that nothing will matter until the major event is under way.

This day at Laytown, some ten years ago, was one of my first assignments with Chris Smith, and it was an education. We didn't back off any of the heady delights of that magical afternoon. A genial steward who took us off to lunch turned out to be a top security judge complete with bodyguard. The fresh-sprouted tented village housed everything from weighing room to sick bay. The course which now basked in the sunshine was ready for us all. Gradually Chris closed on his target. One image, one shuttered moment to sum up the suprise and delight of this unique day at the races. By now we had been tramping for hours. Three races had been run. But it was over in the distance where the perfect picture could be taken. And then only if he cheated just a little.

Oh yes, art has to re-arrange nature sometimes. Just as it was necessary to humour Lester Piggott into posing with the succulent salmon dish, so it was important to charm mother and kids to up bucket and spade and move to the next pool. It seemed a little thing. But it put the sea and posts in perspective. It made the picture.

That's all very wonderful but I can tell you that as a writer it's often something of a mixed blessing. The inspiration of following in Smith's wake can be followed by the humiliation of looking at the photograph and realising that you can't compete.

Jeez, the times I have sat in the night, looking at one of those searingly evocative prints on the other side of the desk, and wondered 'how the hell do we add to that?'

Horse racing is a particularly rich field for the lensman to roam. Firstly because of its vast range of action and atmosphere, of people and places. And secondly because although everyone has a general image of what goes on, both on the track and at the training stable, they have rarely had the chance or taken the trouble to trap what actually makes its special.

In a way racing is a victim of its own easy popularity. The simple involvement of having a bet, of watching your money gallop past, satisfies people's idea of what the sport is all about. But the real fascination has to be much deeper than that – it's actually what is happening out there on the grass. What man and beast are up to when they are at the limit. Exploring that truth in racing is specially important because unlike other major sports, the vast majority of the audience has no practical experience. For instance of the three million people who watched last year's Champion Stakes on Channel 4, only a few thousand would have been on a horse, and the number who had actually ridden in a race would struggle to get into the hundreds. Compare that with an audience for soccer, cricket, rugby or snooker.

But if it's unknown territory it's all the more essential to grab the attention with the image and the way Chris has worked it divides into the atmosphere and the specific. There is only one test for both of them: go out into the country, where the birch flies and the nostrils snort and see if afterwards the pictures evoke and enrich the experience.

To stand at a fence and see the thundering time

capsule of the face sweep up and over is still for me as awesome an experience as when I was first captivated by the glorious challenge all those years ago. For Smith, a travelling eye from other fields it was the natural moment to search for. Down the seasons there have been two other places that always stay in the mind – the athletic explosion of the start and the lapping pool of triumph and disaster that always floods the unsaddling enclosure after a big event. Anyone remotely interested in racing who hasn't taken in the experience has missed the game for real.

Chris Smith didn't miss it. All of us wordsmiths have worn out the typewriter ribbon describing the unique centaur-like genius of Lester Piggot in the saddle. But so much of what has been written is about those last few whip-cracking strides at the finish when even the drunks have come out of the bar to watch. If you want to understand something of the furies which drove Lester right up to his 50th year, to appreciate his dominance of the four legs beneath him, look no further than the picture in this book.

Just the same with the shattered dreams of a great horse in defeat. Nijinsky in the unsaddling enclosure after the Champion Stakes in October, 1972. These scenes are usually a muddled mixture of dismay, disgruntlement and the panting exhaustion of the horse itself. That day at Newmarket, there was all that and more. For just a second the jockey on the ground looked back at the heaving flanks of the massive jangle-nerved bay with whom he had shared and won so much. It was only a glance but, for Lester, it was a speech in itself.

And of course, there is no happiness like taking the saddle off a big winner. Comedy of Errors had always shaped like a champion once the famous

Rimell stable had begun to train him for the hurdling game. But Ken White had begun as just a battler, a journeyman jock. He learnt his trade on moderate horses round the country tracks – Hereford, Worcester, Ludlow, Bangor. It's a rustic, hustling and ruthless way to come. Most get clogged into an earthy but effective style that never develops into the first division. Ken always had to graft, yet he looked the business. He was quiet, modest, genuinely unpretentious. So when his talents finally got recognised he was always vulnerable when the horses ran bad. Men like that don't ever turn nasty, they occasionally get sad. But when it really comes together they have a satisfaction far deeper than the mouthy high-flier. It was like that when Ken White walked away from Comedy of Errors. The smile says more than a lot.

To catch that, to corner the other pictures in this book needs empathy as well as engineering. Of course a 1,000th of a second shutter speed will freeze the moment, but you have got to pick your moment and that also needs a physical alertness so akin to the champions Chris photographs that it's no wonder they get on so well. Smith might be into purity, but when he's in action nobody calls him a pussycat.

One winter day we were at Worcester to cover the first professional ride of future champion Peter Scudamore. We had been up in the Cotswolds at first light, driven on to the races early to check everything. Sometime later another Fleet Street lensman rolled up with the usual line that he was doing the same story, that it was a piece of cake and by the way where were we going to stand for the picture. Smith goes quiet when he's angry, something smouldering in that sandy hair with which wise men never tangle. For a while we continued with our unwanted shadow and took up position by the last fence. No decent shots on the first circuit, but coming towards us for the final time, Scudamore was in front. A picture could be taken. Suddenly there was a yelp of anguish. 'I'm out of film,' moaned our rival. It was a moment when hard men would have 'cocked a deaf'un', even offered a sneering 'hard luck'.

What Chris did was almost worse. With a speed and contempt terrible to behold, he leapt across, siezed the offending camera, changed the film as fast as it takes to write this down, held it out furiously and said one word. 'There'. No, not a pussycat. □

Ken White: Cheltenham 1975

Right, Racing: Cheltenham 1984

Bookmaker: Cheltenham 1984

Right, Steeplechase: Newbury 1976

Lester Piggott: Newmarket 1983

Right, Racing: Newbury 1969

Pat Eddery, Lingfield 1984

Left, Betting: Cheltenham 1984

Lester Piggott and Nijinsky : Newmarket
1972

Right, Jonjo O'Neil and Dawn Run :
Cheltenham 1986

Boat Race: Putney 1967

Hang Gliding: Beachy Head 1985

Manchester United v Liverpool: Goodison
Park 1985

St Helen's v Leeds : Wembley 1972

Above and left, Nicki Lauda : Portuguese
Grand Prix 1984

Boris Becker: Wimbledon 1986

Right, Martina Navratilova: Wimbledon 1987

Swimmer: Olympic Games, Los Angeles
1984